Isle Royale:
Best Park on Earth?

By Dana Whitewater

"In every walk with nature one receives far more than he seeks."
— John Muir

Copyright © 2023

Table of Contents

Dedication

To those with wanderlust in their hearts and dirt on their boots,

For whom every tree whispers secrets and every horizon promises adventure.

Here's to the wild souls, the nature lovers, the explorers.

May the trails always beckon and the beauty of nature forever enchant.

Introduction

The Mystique of Isle Royale: An Overview

Hold onto your hiking boots, folks! Ever heard of an island so bewitching that once you visit, you'll find every other national park... well, just a *tad* less magical? Welcome to Isle Royale, the secret superstar of America's national parks! Nestled in the frosty embrace of Lake Superior, this remote gem has been playing hard-to-get with travelers for years. And, oh boy, does it play the game well! A bewitching blend of wilderness wonder, this island teases with tales of wolves, whispers of wildflowers, and the promise of pure, unadulterated adventure.

Why Isle Royale Stands Out Among National Parks

Now, we've all got our favorite national park stories. The bear that stole your sandwich in Yosemite. The time you almost lost your hat to a gusty wind in the Grand Canyon. Or that utterly gorgeous sunrise in Acadia that you Instagrammed the heck out of. But Isle Royale? It's like the cool indie band of the national park world: not everyone's heard of it, but those who have can't stop raving! It isn't just a park; it's an experience. No cars, no bustling crowds, just you, Mother Nature, and a serene wilderness that feels like a world apart. And let's not forget its exclusive fan club of moose and wolves, who, rumor has it, throw some wild parties under the northern lights!

Why You Want to Visit Isle Royale

Still not convinced? Alright, picture this: a day spent kayaking in the shimmering waters, followed by a hike where every turn reveals a view that makes you gasp louder than the last time you stepped on a rogue LEGO. As night falls, you're cozied up by a campfire, roasting marshmallows, and wondering if the Milky Way has always been this... *dazzling*. Whether you're a hardcore backpacker, a casual nature lover, or someone just looking for a digital detox, Isle Royale serves up a slice of heaven with a side of adventure. And trust us, after a visit here, your travel tales will be the stuff of legends at every dinner party!

Pack your bags, tie those laces, and let's dive deep into the mystic realm of Isle Royale, the *undeniable* best park on Earth. Ready? Let's go!

Chapter 1: The History of Isle Royale

Early Inhabitants and Archaeological Finds

"Once upon a time" isn't just the beginning of fairy tales; it's how we kick off our historical journey to Isle Royale! And this tale? It's older than your grandma's secret cookie recipe. Our story starts with the Native Americans who, drawn by the allure of Isle Royale, came, saw, and totally adored! Archaeologists have had a field day (pun intended) uncovering ancient copper mining sites, remnants of tools, and pottery pieces, suggesting the island's popularity even thousands of years ago. Sure, there were no hipster cafes back then, but with its rich resources and stunning vistas, who needed one?

The Path to Becoming a National Park

From Native American hotspot to a national treasure, Isle Royale's transformation is no less epic than a Hollywood blockbuster! The early 20th century saw a rising chorus of voices saying, "Hey, this place is special!" (or, you know, something to that effect). It wasn't just its beauty, but also its unique ecosystem that captured imaginations. And so, with a flourish of a pen and a lot of elbow grease, in 1940, Isle Royale was knighted as a National Park. Roll out the green carpet, everyone!

Key Figures in Isle Royale's History

While the moose and wolves might like to think they're the island's biggest celebrities, some two-legged folks have left their mark too:

- **Albert Stoll Jr.**: Think of him as the park's guardian angel! As the editor of Detroit News, he campaigned fiercely for Isle Royale's National Park status. He probably dreamt of starry nights and the call of loons more than we'll ever know.

- **John M. Longyear**: Not just a cool surname, but a cooler legacy! An industrialist who once owned land on the island, he later donated it, ensuring its protection. Talk about a plot twist!

Famous People Who Have Visited the Park

Isle Royale's guestbook is no joke. Some cool cats who've wandered its trails include:

- **Ernest Hemingway**: Rumor has it, he came here fishing for trout and inspiration. Given his literary genius, we'd say he found both in abundance!

- **Teddy Roosevelt**: Our nature-loving president was no stranger to America's wild spaces. Isle Royale's rugged charm? Just Teddy's cup of tea!

And who knows? By the end of your trip, you might just add your name to this list of legends who've fallen under the Isle Royale spell.

And there we have it, folks! A whirlwind history tour of Isle Royale. From its ancient residents to modern-day admirers, this island has been wowing audiences for ages. And we're just getting started!

Chapter 2: The Unique Geography

Formation of the Island

Alright, geography buffs, it's time to geek out! Isle Royale didn't just pop up like a jack-in-the-box. No, sir! It was more of a slow-cook situation. Millions (yep, you read that right) of years ago, volcanic activity was like, "Let's make an island!" Lava flowed, hardening and layering to create what we now recognize as Isle Royale. Over the years, the island has witnessed quite a bit of drama - from tectonic shifts to fiery eruptions. It's safe to say Isle Royale has a backstory that could rival any superhero origin tale!

Glacial Impact and the Shaping of the Land

Enter the Ice Age and our chilly protagonist: glaciers! These massive sheets of ice were the ultimate landscape designers, bulldozing their way through and sculpting the land. As they advanced and retreated, the glaciers carved valleys, created ridges, and left behind those sparkly lakes and ponds we adore. Thanks to these icy influencers, Isle Royale got its iconic rugged appearance. Imagine a natural facelift that took thousands of years!

The Surrounding Waters: Lake Superior's Role

Ah, Lake Superior – the grand dame of the Great Lakes and Isle Royale's protective guardian! Now, this isn't just any lake. It's the largest freshwater lake by surface area in the world. Go big or go home, right?

Lake Superior plays a massive role (literally) in Isle Royale's life. From influencing the island's climate (mild summers and not-so-harsh winters) to being a highway for various species (hello, fishy friends!), Lake Superior is Isle Royale's BFF. Its waters have also been the backdrop for countless adventures, shipwrecks, and tales of maritime lore. Oh, and let's not forget those mood-lifting sunrises and sunsets that leave visitors spellbound!

And that's a wrap on our deep dive (pun very much intended) into Isle Royale's geography! From its volcanic beginnings to its icy makeovers and its bond with Lake Superior, Isle Royale is proof that Mother Nature truly is the world's best artist. Ready for the next chapter in our island saga? Onward, fellow explorer!

Chapter 3: Flora and Fauna

Iconic Species: From Moose to Wolves

Roll out the red carpet, nature lovers! It's time to meet Isle Royale's celebrity residents: the moose and the wolves. Our first star, the moose, made a grand entrance around the early 1900s. With long legs built for wading, a love for munching on aquatic plants, and those unforgettable antlers, moose are like the cool, laid-back surfers of the island.

Then, in the late 1940s, the wolves crashed the party, making their way to Isle Royale across an ice bridge from Canada. These canines brought drama, action, and a whole lot of howling. Their relationship with the moose? It's complicated! Sometimes they're predators; sometimes they're just distant neighbors. Their dynamic dance is a living soap opera, keeping scientists and wildlife enthusiasts on their toes.

The Island's Vegetation: Forests, Ferns, and More

But it's not all about the big names. Isle Royale's green scene is a botanical bonanza! The island boasts lush forests with spruce, fir, birch, and aspen trees, creating a canopy that's the envy of other national parks. Then, there's the understory – a vibrant mix of ferns, wildflowers, and berry bushes, painting the ground in every shade of green, purple, yellow, and red.

Stroll around, and you might find yourself amidst thickets of thimbleberries (yum!) or stumbling upon fragrant patches of wild orchids. From the sun-dappled woods to the serene wetlands, every nook of Isle Royale is a testament to nature's botanical brilliance.

The Delicate Ecosystem Balance

But here's the tea: Isle Royale's ecosystem is like a finely tuned orchestra. Every plant, every creature has a role to play, and it's all about balance. The moose munch on the vegetation, the wolves keep the moose population in check, and the plants provide food and shelter to countless creatures.

But like any delicate system, it's vulnerable. Climate change, invasive species, and human interference can throw things off-kilter. The good news? With conservation efforts and responsible tourism, we can ensure that Isle Royale's symphony of life plays on for generations to come.

Well, wasn't that a wild ride? From show-stopping mammals to the unsung heroes of the plant world and the intricate web of life that binds them all, Isle Royale is a living, breathing masterpiece. Ready to delve deeper into this island of wonders? Stick around; the adventure's just getting started!

Chapter 4: Hiking and Exploration

Best Trails for Different Skill Levels

Tie those laces tight because it's time to hit the trails! Whether you're a newbie with fresh hiking boots or a seasoned explorer with stories for days, Isle Royale has a path for you:

- **For the Beginners**: *Stoll Memorial Trail* is your jam! A breezy 2-mile loop offering lake views, and if you listen closely, the lake might just whisper some of its secrets!

- **Intermediate Hikers, Assemble**: *Greenstone Ridge Trail* is calling! It's the spine of the island, and while you won't bump into any chiropractors, you'll surely get a dose of mesmerizing views.

- **Expert Trailblazers**: Dive into the *Minong Ridge Trail*. It's challenging, it's wild, and it's an unforgettable experience that'll earn you some serious bragging rights.

Hidden Gems and Lesser-Known Routes

But hey, maybe you're the kind who loves the road less traveled? Isle Royale's got your back:

- **Daisy Farm Trail**: Wander among the remnants of old mining sites and think of the days when the quest for copper was all the rage.

- **Rock Harbor Lighthouse Trail**: It's not just about the destination, but oh, what a destination it is! This trail culminates in a historic lighthouse with tales as old as time.

Safety Tips and Preparation for the Wilderness

Adventure's fun, but safety's number one!

1. **Stay Hydrated**: That water bottle isn't just a cool accessory. Drink up!

2. **Map It Out**: Always have a map and compass. GPS is cool, but old-school navigation is foolproof.

3. **Dress Smart**: Layers, folks! Isle Royale's weather can be more unpredictable than a season finale cliffhanger.

4. **Wildlife Wisdom**: Remember, this is the home of wolves and moose. Admire from a distance.

5. **Leave No Trace**: Pack out what you pack in. The island thanks you in advance!

Bigfoot Sightings

Now, here's where things get *hairy* (literally!). Whispered tales and blurry photos have made rounds claiming Bigfoot's vacationing on Isle Royale. While no concrete evidence exists (and park rangers might chuckle at the idea), the legends persist. Some say it's just tall tales spun by campfires, while others swear by mysterious footprints. Who knows? Maybe Bigfoot's just another hiker, looking for some peace and quiet. Keep those eyes peeled, and cameras ready!

And that's the wrap on Isle Royale's hiking and exploration scene! Whether you're seeking well-trodden paths, hidden wonders, or perhaps a glimpse of the elusive Bigfoot, this island promises adventures aplenty. Ready to lace up and explore? The trails await!

Chapter 5: Water Adventures

Kayaking, Canoeing, and Boating Around Isle Royale

Ahoy, water babies! When surrounded by the pristine blue of Lake Superior, it's only natural to want to dive (or paddle) right in:

- **Kayaking**: Glide through the serene bays and coves, with hidden inlets beckoning you for a closer look. Got an afternoon? Explore Tobin Harbor. Got a day? Circle around Raspberry Island. Just you, the rhythmic paddle strokes, and maybe a curious otter or two!

- **Canoeing**: Traverse the island's inland waterways! Places like Siskiwit Lake offer a different perspective of Isle Royale, with calm waters reflecting the sky and forests alike.

- **Boating**: For those who prefer a bit more horsepower, boating around Isle Royale provides panoramic views of its rugged coastline. Just remember: with great horsepower comes great responsibility. Watch out for shallow areas and be mindful of the environment.

Prime Fishing Spots and What to Catch

Ready to channel your inner angler? Let's talk fishing:

- **Hot Spots**: Popular spots include Moskey Basin, Rock Harbor, and Lane Cove. Whether from the shore or a boat, the fish are waiting!

- **What's Biting**: From juicy Northern Pike to Lake Trout, the waters are teeming. And if you're lucky, you might just hook the elusive Brook Trout in some of the inland lakes.

Pro tip: Always check local regulations and get the necessary permits. Isle Royale's fish are cool, but the park rangers? They mean business!

Snorkeling and Diving: Discovering the Underwater World

Who says the magic is only on land? Dive beneath the waves and discover a world of wonder:

- **Snorkeling**: Crystal-clear waters mean visibility galore. Spot ancient geological formations, curious fish, and maybe even a historic artifact or two.

- **Diving**: Isle Royale is a graveyard of shipwrecks, making it a diver's dream. Explore underwater relics like the SS America or the Emperor. As you dive into history, remember to respect these sites - they're a testament to the lake's power and tales of old.

Splash! That's the sound of endless adventures awaiting you in and around the waters of Isle Royale. Whether paddling, fishing, or diving deep, there's a splashy escapade with your name on it. Dive in and let the water tales begin!

Chapter 6: Stargazing and the Northern Lights

Isle Royale's Dark Sky Designation

Let's kick things off with some stellar news (pun totally intended)! Isle Royale has been dubbed a Dark Sky Park. But what's that, you ask? It means the island has one of the cleanest, darkest, and most star-studded skies out there. No glaring city lights, no neon billboards – just pure, unadulterated celestial beauty. On a clear night, the Milky Way doesn't just make an appearance; it steals the show!

Tips for Night Sky Photography

Want to capture the stars and take a slice of the night home with you? Here's your cheat sheet:

1. **Steady Does It**: Use a tripod. The Earth might feel still, but it's always moving, and a tripod will keep things sharp.

2. **Go Wide and Slow**: A wide-angle lens and a slow shutter speed will capture more of the starry spectacle.

3. **Manual Mode is Your Friend**: Auto-focus at night? Not so hot. Switch to manual, focus on a bright star or distant light, and then get snapping!

4. **ISO Balance**: A higher ISO captures more light, but too high, and things get grainy. Experiment to find your sweet spot.

The Magic of the Aurora Borealis

If stars are the regular cast of Isle Royale's nightly show, the Northern Lights are the surprise guest stars that leave everyone spellbound. Dancing hues of green, pink, and purple paint the sky, making it look like Mother Nature's personal canvas. The best part? Isle Royale's northern location and clear skies make it one of the best seats in the house for this ethereal performance.

UFOs, Shooting Stars, and Other Unexplained Phenomena in the Sky

But wait, there's more! Every once in a while, the skies above Isle Royale serve up something extra mysterious:

- **Shooting Stars**: Also known as meteor showers, these are nature's fireworks. Make a wish, or ten!

- **UFO Sightings**: Now, we're not saying it's aliens... but it's aliens. Kidding! (Or are we?) There have been occasional reports of unidentified flying objects. Whether they're extraterrestrial or just unusual, they add to the island's mystique.

- **Mysterious Lights**: Sometimes, lights appear on the horizon, dancing and darting. They could be distant boats, planes, or maybe, just maybe, something a bit more... unexplained.

So, night owls and space nerds, rejoice! Isle Royale's nightly displays, from shimmering stars to the elusive Northern Lights, and the odd UFO, promise a celestial experience that's out of this world. Grab a blanket, lay back, and let the universe work its magic.

Chapter 7: Cultural and Historical Sites

Lighthouses and Maritime History

Step aside, skyscrapers! Isle Royale's lighthouses have been standing tall and proud for decades, guiding sailors and captivating visitors. The *Rock Harbor Lighthouse* and *Windigo Visitor Center* offer glimpses into maritime history. With tales of stormy nights, brave lighthouse keepers, and ships that narrowly escaped the clutches of Lake Superior, these iconic structures are a beacon (literally!) of the island's storied past.

Native American Sites and Their Significance

Long before it became a national park, Isle Royale was a sacred space for Native Americans. Sites like ancient copper mines hint at the island's significance as a resource hub. But more than that, spiritual sites and artifacts paint a picture of a land deeply revered. When exploring, remember: these aren't just historical sites; they're a testament to a rich cultural tapestry that predates us by millennia.

Mining and Early Settlements

Think of the Gold Rush but swap gold for copper! In the 1800s, Isle Royale was buzzing with miners dreaming of striking it rich. Old mines and settlements like *McCargoe Cove* give us a peek into a time when life was rugged, risks were high, and the island's copper was the hottest ticket in town.

Funny Stories About the Park in History

Every good history lesson needs a chuckle or two, right? Isle Royale doesn't disappoint:

- **Moose vs. Mail**: Legend has it, a park ranger once had a standoff with a moose that took a keen interest in the mail delivery boat. Maybe it was waiting for a package?

- **The Great Berry Battle**: Two settlers once laid claim to the same berry patch, leading to a hilarious "berry-off" where they competed to see who could pick the most berries. Spoiler: the real winners were the pies baked afterward.

- **Fishy Business**: An old journal entry from a fisherman on the island lamented about catching too many fish. His solution? Taking a nap and hoping the fish would be less bitey afterward. If only all problems were that delightful!

From the solemn echoes of ancient cultures to the misadventures of settlers and quirky tales that have withstood the test of time, Isle Royale's history is as vast and varied as its landscapes. Each site, each story adds a layer to the rich tapestry of an island that has seen and heard it all. Ready for more tales and trails? Onwards, history buffs and adventure seekers!

Chapter 8: Seasonal Wonders

Spring Blooms and Migrating Birds

Spring on Isle Royale is like nature's grand opening act after a winter intermission. Flowers timidly poke their heads out, with trilliums and wild orchids leading the charge. But it's not just the ground that's buzzing with life. Look up, and you might spot migratory birds winging their way north. Warblers sing their heart out, raptors soar with newfound vigor, and the island becomes a birdwatcher's paradise.

Summer's Warmth and Water Activities

Ah, summer! The time when Isle Royale truly shines (and not just because of the sun). The waters of Lake Superior beckon adventurers for kayaking, canoeing, and those daring dives off cliffs into the refreshing deep blue. It's the season of long hikes, campfire stories, and those magic moments when the golden hour paints everything in a hue of adventure.

Fall Foliage and Tranquility

If summer is a lively party, fall is the poetic afterparty. The trees don an array of colors, making every trail a walk through an artist's palette. Reds, oranges, yellows – it's as if the forests are giving one last spectacular show before the curtain of winter. The crowds thin out, and the tranquility deepens, making it a perfect time for reflection, both in the calm waters of the inland lakes and in one's soul.

The Solitude of Winter (Even Though the Park is Closed in Winter)

Now, here's the thing. While the park officially shuts its doors in winter, the island doesn't just disappear. It transforms. Blanketed in snow, with frozen waters shimmering under the pale winter sun, Isle Royale in winter is a sight to behold from afar. It's a season of quiet, of introspection. The wolves tread softly on the snow, moose forage, and the island waits, in serene solitude, for the cycle to begin anew.

Isle Royale's beauty isn't static; it evolves with every season, offering visitors a unique experience each time. Whether you're basking in the summer sun, marveling at the fall colors, or dreaming of the winter stillness, Isle Royale promises a wonder-filled embrace. Ready for more wonders? Keep turning the pages; the journey continues!

Chapter 9: Sustainable Tourism and Conservation

The Importance of Leave No Trace Principles

You know the feeling of walking into a pristine room? The scent of freshness, everything in its place? That's the feeling nature should evoke every single time. The Leave No Trace principles aren't just guidelines; they're a pact between humans and nature. Whether it's packing out your trash, not picking plants, or staying on the trail, these principles ensure that Isle Royale remains as untouched and magical for future generations as it was for those before us. It's all about taking only memories and leaving only footprints, not carbon ones!

The Role of Park Rangers and Conservation Efforts

Heroes don't always wear capes; sometimes, they wear ranger hats! Isle Royale's park rangers are the unsung guardians of its vast expanse. From conducting research on the delicate balance between wolves and moose to guiding awe-inspired visitors, they're the bridge between humans and nature. Their conservation efforts, from habitat restoration to monitoring wildlife health, ensure that Isle Royale remains a thriving ecosystem. A nod of gratitude, a shared story, or a heartfelt thank you goes a long way in recognizing their tireless dedication.

How Visitors Can Make a Positive Impact

Believe it or not, every visitor holds the power to be a conservationist! Here's how:

1. **Educate Before You Visit**: Familiarize yourself with the island's unique ecology, so you know what to expect and how to behave.

2. **Respect Wildlife**: Remember, you're a guest in their home. Maintain a safe distance and avoid feeding any animals.

3. **Reduce, Reuse, Recycle**: Minimize waste, especially plastic. Bring reusable containers and bags.

4. **Join a Volunteer Program**: Many programs allow visitors to actively participate in conservation work, from trail maintenance to data collection.

5. **Spread the Word**: Share the beauty and importance of Isle Royale with others, but also emphasize the importance of sustainable practices.

Embracing sustainability isn't just a trend; it's a promise to the land that has given so much. Isle Royale, with its majestic beauty and delicate ecosystems, deserves nothing less than our utmost respect and care. Here's to leaving a legacy of love, responsibility, and active conservation for the national parks that have captured our hearts. Let's pave the way for a brighter, greener future!

Chapter 10: Romance in the Park

Romantic Spots for Picnicking or More

Love is in the air! Or is that the scent of wildflowers? Either way, Isle Royale has no shortage of romantic hideaways:

- **Hidden Lake Overlook**: With a view overlooking the serene Hidden Lake and surrounded by lush forest, it's a spot straight out of a romance novel. Lay out a blanket, pop open that picnic basket, and let nature provide the soundtrack.

- **Scoville Point**: Imagine this – a gentle breeze, the sound of waves lapping, and a panoramic view of Lake Superior as you both share a meal and heart-to-heart talks.

- **Grace Creek Overlook**: Nestled away from the main trails, this spot offers tranquility, seclusion, and a stunning backdrop for a romantic meal.

Best Places to Propose Marriage

Thinking of popping the question? Here are the ultimate spots that guarantee a (hopefully!) resounding "YES!":

- **Mount Ojibway Tower**: Elevate your proposal, literally! With a 360-degree view of the park, it's hard not to feel on top of the world. Plus, that hike up is the perfect metaphor for the journey you're embarking on together.

- **Sunset at Rock Harbor**: As the sky bursts into hues of orange, pink, and purple, take that deep breath and ask the most important question of your life.

- **By the Stoll Trail Shipwreck**: For the couples who love a touch of history and mystery, this underwater relic offers a unique backdrop for a proposal.

Best Trails to Steal a Kiss from Your Significant Other

Cheeky, aren't we? Here's where you can sneak in that romantic moment:

- **Minong Mine Trail**: Not only is it a relatively less-traveled trail, ensuring some privacy, but the remnants of the old Minong Mine add a touch of adventurous charm.

- **Lookout Louise**: A moderate hike leads to this stunning viewpoint. As you catch your breath from the hike (or the view), lean in for a memorable kiss.

- **Huginnin Cove**: A trail that offers secluded spots, beautiful vistas, and plenty of opportunities for a quick romantic rendezvous.

Love and nature, a match made in heaven! Whether you're looking to start your romantic journey, celebrate years of togetherness, or simply enjoy each other's company in nature's embrace, Isle Royale offers the perfect backdrop. Here's to love stories penned under starry skies, whispered amidst rustling leaves, and celebrated with the grandeur of Mother Nature as the witness!

Chapter 11: Planning Your Visit

Best Times to Visit and How to Reach

When it comes to Isle Royale, timing is everything!

- **Best Times**: Late spring to early fall (May to September) offers the best weather. However, for fewer crowds and a serene experience, consider late September to early October.

- **Getting There**: Isle Royale is an island, which means no road access! Your options include:

    o **By Ferry**: Multiple services run from both Michigan and Minnesota. Choose based on your itinerary and starting point.

    o **By Seaplane**: For those looking for a quicker (and more scenic) route, seaplanes operate from Houghton, Michigan.

Accommodations: From Campsites to Lodges

- **Campsites**: Isle Royale boasts numerous campgrounds. Whether you prefer the lakeside ambiance of *Three Mile* or the forested beauty of *Lane Cove*, there's a spot for every camper. Remember to get a permit!

- **Lodges**: If camping isn't your style, fear not! *Rock Harbor Lodge* offers comfortable accommodations with the bonus of gorgeous lake views.

Packing Essentials and Preparing for Your Trip

- **Map and Compass**: Because sometimes, going old school is the best way to navigate.

- **Water Treatment Supplies**: While the island has freshwater sources, it's essential to filter or treat the water.

- **First Aid Kit**: For those minor oops moments.

- **Multi-tool or Knife**: You never know when it'll come in handy!

- **Bug Spray and Sunscreen**: Because bugs and sunburns? Not so romantic.

What to Wear

Dress not just to impress, but also for success!

- **Layer Up**: Temperatures can fluctuate, so layers are your best friends.

- **Waterproof Footwear**: Sturdy, comfortable, and preferably waterproof hiking boots will make those treks enjoyable.

- **Rain Gear**: Because Mother Nature can sometimes be unpredictable.

- **Hat and Sunglasses**: Protect yourself from the sun in style.

What Not to Bring

Keep it light and eco-friendly!

- **Plastic**: Minimize single-use plastic. Opt for reusable containers and bottles.

- **Perishable Food**: Without proper storage, it spoils quickly. Plus, it might attract unwanted wildlife.

- **Loud Music Players**: The sound of nature is music enough.

- **Pets**: As much as you might want to share the experience with your furry friend, pets aren't allowed in order to protect the island's ecosystem.

There you have it, future Isle Royale adventurer! With a little prep and a sprinkle of anticipation, your trip to this pristine paradise promises to be everything you've dreamed of and more. From the moment you set foot (or paddle) onto the island to the tales you'll carry home, get ready for an unforgettable journey. Happy planning and even happier exploring!

Conclusion

Isle Royale's Legacy and the Future of the Park

Isle Royale is more than just an island; it's a living testament to the timeless dance between nature and time. From its ancient geological formations to the symphony of life it supports, the island stands as a beacon of natural beauty and resilience. But with the changing global environment, Isle Royale's future, like many natural wonders, is at a crossroads.

Conservation, research, and responsible tourism play a pivotal role in preserving the island's legacy. The national park status isn't just a designation; it's a commitment — a promise to protect, cherish, and uphold the sanctity of this natural marvel for generations to come.

Personal Reflections on the Isle Royale Experience

Words often fall short in encapsulating the essence of Isle Royale. It's an experience — a heady mix of adventure, wonder, introspection, and connection. To walk its trails is to step into a story millions of years in the making. To listen to the call of a loon or the howl of a wolf is to hear the melodies of raw, untamed nature. To gaze upon its starlit skies or witness the magic of the Northern Lights is to be humbled and awed.

Each visitor carries back a piece of Isle Royale within them, be it in the form of memories, tales, or a renewed appreciation for the natural world. And in return, they leave behind a part of their spirit, woven into the very fabric of the island.

As this book comes to a close, the journey, in many ways, is just beginning. Isle Royale isn't just a destination; it's an invitation — to explore, to learn, to feel, and most importantly, to connect. Here's to the paths less traveled, to the stories waiting to be told, and to the timeless allure of Isle Royale. May its magic continue to inspire, today, tomorrow, and always.